A Crabtree Branches Book

Improving Your Social Skills

DON'T BE A BULLY

VICKY BUREAU

Crabtree Publishing
crabtreebooks.com

School-to-Home Support for Caregivers and Teachers

This high-interest book is designed to motivate striving students with engaging topics while building fluency, vocabulary, and an interest in reading. Here are a few questions and activities to help the reader build upon his or her comprehension skills.

Before Reading:

- *What do I think this book is about?*
- *What do I know about this topic?*
- *What do I want to learn about this topic?*
- *Why am I reading this book?*

During Reading:

- *I wonder why...*
- *I'm curious to know...*
- *How is this like something I already know?*
- *What have I learned so far?*

After Reading:

- *What was the author trying to teach me?*
- *What are some details?*
- *How did the photographs and captions help me understand more?*
- *Read the book again and look for the vocabulary words.*
- *What questions do I still have?*

Extension Activities:

- *What was your favorite part of the book? Write a paragraph on it.*
- *Draw a picture of your favorite thing you learned from the book.*

TABLE OF CONTENTS

WHAT IS A BULLY?

What does the word **bully** mean to you?

We all make bad choices sometimes. We may say or do something unkind. Does that make you a bully? One unkind act does not make a bully. An apology can make that right.

A bully is someone who tries to hurt, scare, or embarrass others on purpose. A bully will act this way over and over again without being **provoked**. They will also try to make you feel powerless to stop it.

UNDERSTANDING EMOTIONS

Have you ever felt so angry, sad, or excited that you acted in a way that could hurt others? Let's talk about **emotions** and how **extreme** emotions can lead to behaviors that can hurt others.

We all feel emotions. These are the feelings that we experience throughout the day. Emotions play an important role in how we behave. However, when we experience extreme emotions, sometimes it is hard to calm down and do or say the right thing.

DID YOU KNOW?

When you get stuck in a pattern of negative behavior, ask for help to turn that pattern into positive behavior.

WHAT MAKES A BULLY?

No one is born a bully. There are many reasons people become bullies. Some people want to feel powerful or important. Some don't care about, or have trouble understanding, the feelings of others. Some bullies learned this behavior when they were bullied themselves.

When somebody experiences extreme emotions and does not know how to stop them or get help, that person may find themselves feeling frustrated, lonely, angry, sad, or overly excited. These emotions can lead to bullying behavior to make the person feel in control again.

DID YOU KNOW?

Seeking the help of someone else when you are being bullied significantly decreases the likelihood of conflict.

CHECKPOINT: TEST YOUR SKILLS

What is the difference between an emotion and an extreme emotion?

Have you ever experienced an extreme emotion?

What happened to cause it? How did it make others around you feel? How did it make you feel?

ANGER

Let's explore some feelings that can turn into extreme emotions.

What makes you feel angry?

Anger describes the emotion of displeasure or annoyance, especially when someone feels out of control. When somebody is angry, they can say or do things that are hurtful. In most cases, the feeling of anger is temporary and does not last long. When someone feels better and is less angry, they may apologize or try to make things better. However, extreme anger can cause someone to act like a bully.

DID YOU KNOW?

Words like rage, fury, and tantrum are all associated with the emotion of extreme anger.

SADNESS

Let's explore another feeling that can turn into an extreme emotion.

What makes you feel sad?

Sadness describes the emotion of feeling sorrow after something negative has occurred. When someone is sad, they can seem distant and hopeless. When someone experiences extreme sadness, they may act withdrawn or push friends away. Extreme sadness can also cause someone to act like a bully.

DID YOU KNOW?

Depression is a feeling of extreme sadness and hopelessness. People who are depressed should seek help from others.

FRUSTRATION

Let's explore another feeing that can turn into an extreme emotion.

What makes you feel frustrated?

Frustration describes the emotion you experience when things are not going as planned. When someone is frustrated, they feel as though they cannot help themselves. When someone experiences extreme frustration, they may feel powerless and may even want to give up. They may act out and yell. Extreme frustration can cause someone to act like a bully.

DID YOU KNOW?

Breathing exercises can significantly decrease the likelihood of conflict when someone is frustrated. Try it!

ELATION

Let's explore another feeling that can turn into an extreme emotion.

What makes you feel elated?

Elation describes the emotion of being so happy or excited that it is beyond a person's control. When someone is elated, they may have a hard time remaining calm or understanding their body language. They may also have a hard time controlling their thoughts or actions. Extreme elation can cause someone to act like a bully.

CHECKPOINT: TEST YOUR SKILLS

How have you helped yourself calm down when you feel an extreme emotion?

Have you ever talked with a friend who was experiencing an extreme emotion? Did it help calm that person?

If bullies join together to make someone feel bad, do you think it's possible to join with others to make someone feel good?

DID YOU KNOW?

All school counselors in the United States are certified by the American School Counseling Association.

HOW TO HELP YOURSELF

You may have experienced extreme emotions at times. Maybe your brother accidentally broke your favorite toy and you felt extremely angry. Or maybe your dog got very sick and you felt extremely sad. Maybe it was the day of your birthday party and you felt extremely elated.

In most cases, feeling extreme emotions is normal and doesn't usually last very long. But if you experience extreme emotions a lot or if you feel like you can't make them go away, you may need to ask a grown-up for help. Your **school counselor** is someone who is specially trained to work with you and help you understand your emotions.

HOW TO HELP OTHERS

You may have experienced someone else's extreme emotions. Maybe your classmate screamed at you after you broke his favorite pencil. Maybe you made a card for a friend after their goldfish died.

We can **support** people around us who are showing extreme emotions by letting them know we are there for them. But if you see that someone you know experiences extreme emotions a lot, or can't seem to make them go away, the best way to support that person is by talking to your school counselor.

THE CYCLE OF BULLYING

We all learn behavior by watching the people around us. If we are not surrounded by people who know how to control their extreme emotions, then it is difficult to learn how to control our own. Sometimes this makes people who have been bullied act like a bully themselves.

When this happens, it is called a cycle of bullying.

Let's think of an example:

Tommy is the youngest of four brothers. His older brothers pick on him a lot. They shove him out of the way to use the bathroom, and they call him names. Tommy doesn't tell his mom because he is afraid they will only pick on him more and call him a baby if he 'tattle-tells.'

When Tommy comes to school, he is the biggest kid in his class. He picks on others and acts like a bully because he is used to it at home.

IT'S OK
TO ASK
for
HELP

BREAKING THE CYCLE OF BULLYING

Tommy's story is an example of the cycle of bullying. He feels extremely hurt, scared, and powerless over his brothers. This leads to him feeling extreme anger, sadness, and frustration. When Tommy comes to school feeling these extreme emotions, he is likely to act out because he is not thinking clearly.

You can help Tommy, and you can help yourself!

If you or someone you know experiences extreme emotions that lead to negative behavior, talk to your school counselor. He or she can show you ways to help you control overwhelming emotions and make better decisions. You can support yourself and others during times of extreme emotions and help break the cycle of bullying.

GLOSSARY

anger (ANG·ger): A strong feeling of displeasure and annoyance

bully (BU·lee): A person who repeats behavior intended to hurt and to gain power over a victim

cycle of bullying (SAI·kl uhv BU·lee·ing): A series of events that leads someone who was bullied to become a bully themselves

elation (ee·LAY·shn): A feeling of joy and pride

emotions (ee·MOW·shinz): Feelings, including joy, sorrow, fear, anger, love

extreme (ek·STREEM): To a very great degree, far from average

frustration (fruh·STRAY·shun): A feeling of anger at not being able to complete something

provoked (pruh-VOHKT): To have been incited or stirred up

sadness (SAD·nuhs): A feeling of pain or loss

school counselor (skool KOWN·se·ler): An adult at school you can go to when you need help

support (suh·PORT): Providing comfort and resources

INDEX

WEBSITES TO VISIT

www.stopbullying.gov

www.pacerkidsagainstbullying.org/#/home

www.pbs.org/inthemix/shows/show_bullying_whattodo.html

ABOUT THE AUTHOR

Vicky Bureau was born in Longueuil, Quebec, and was raised in South Florida. As a teacher, she developed a passion for the social and emotional growth of her students and later transitioned into the area of child and adolescent psychology after earning her master's degree in school counseling. In addition to working with children, Vicky loves to be surrounded by animals and nature. She lives in Fort Lauderdale with her family: Billy, Khloe, M.J., and Max; her three cats, Alley, Baguette, and Salem; and her dog, Boomer.

Written by: Vicky Bureau
Cover designed by: Rhea Magaro Wallace
Interior designed by: Kathy Walsh
Series Development: James Earley
Proofreader: Kathy Middleton
Educational Consultant: Marie Lemke M.Ed.

Photographs: Shutterstock Cover robert_s, Viktoriia Protsak, LightField Studios; Background robert_s; Color Splash Viktoriia Protsak, Box p 7, 9, 13, 15, 17, 22 Puwadol Jaturawutthichai; p 5 Africa Studio; p7 Photographee.eu; p 9 Lopolo; p 11 Jan H Andersen; p 13 Lopolo; p 15 Monkey Business Images; p 17 michaeljung; p 19 MANDY GODBEHEAR; p 21 Timof; p 22 VH-studio; p 24 SynthEx; p 26 Savicic; p 28 Photographee.eu

Crabtree Publishing

crabtreebooks.com 800-387-7650

Printed in the U.S.A./012023/CG20220815

Published in Canada
Crabtree Publishing
616 Welland Ave.
St. Catharines, Ontario
L2M 5V6

Published in the United States
Crabtree Publishing
347 Fifth Ave
Suite 1402-145
New York, NY 10016

Library and Archives Canada Cataloguing in Publication
Available at Library and Archives Canada

Library of Congress Cataloging-in-Publication Data
Available at the Library of Congress

Hardcover: 978-1-0396-6045-8
Paperback: 978-1-0396-6240-7
Ebook (pdf): 978-1-0396-7036-5
Epub: 978-1-0396-7234-5